to

Ren

from

Bridge Green
Farm Girl

Very best
wishes

Caroline

Simmons

So lovely to know
your

ie Jue Pond.

First published 2016
Catberry Press
Lowestoft

9780995478114

Polly's family

From the very time that Polly was born, her parents and family made her feel completely safe, making her feel wanted, treasured, responsible and needed. She was made to feel that she could trust them and if or when anything happened they would be there to make certain that no harm came to her. She understood that she was needed and wanted, and not a bother to anyone, making this early assurance for her in life.

Hers was a family with pride and discipline, expecting of her no more or less than would have been possible at whatever age she might be. At the same time, discipline was very strict, there were no reservations there.

Equally, because Polly was able to hold a conversation at a very young age, at two years everybody could understand her, like-wise she understood them. Her parents were very patient with her from a young age as she was very sensitive, inquiring and capable of understanding situations as they arose.

There is an expression that you can't put an old head on young shoulders, but in fact that is what actually happened. Polly was expected to understand and be understood and everything was very clear. Yes always meant yes and no meant no, which represented security. This enabled Polly to grow up and mature very quickly. A lot was expected of her, especially good behaviour, that was a must.

Preparing the Ground

It is a lovely October morning. Stormer the horse is pulling the plough, his strength and his power showing in all his muscles, the plough cutting deep into clay soil where this same practice has been recurring, turning over for hundreds, even thousands, of years. It will be ready for the winter wheat which will follow in next year's rotation of crops. This same process is repeated each day until the five acres is finished. Man, horse and plough walk seven or eleven miles in each day.

Looking After the Land

Through the top of the field as they are nearing, the man guiding the horse spots a little black and white dog coming through a gap in the hedge. Quite a few more steps, maybe six or seven minutes later, a tiny little girl appears in the same gap. Quite some time later horse and ploughman reach the same spot, stopping and waiting for the old grandfather who is coming along with the mid-morning ploughman's dinner and can of tea. This is a regular occurrence on the farm when getting the land ready for next year's crops.

There is, of course, a nosebag of food that's ready for Stormer.

Everyone sits down on the bank to partake of the bread and cheese, of which the ploughman shares a slight portion with his small daughter, who isn't able to run as fast as Jack the dog, and grandfather, now into his late seventies, walks very slowly indeed, eventually each in turn arrive.

Adults talk of wonderful autumn weather, the sound of birds, mostly crows, rooks and pigeons, as most of the smaller birds have migrated now.

These men take guidance from the birds, animals, and clouds in the sky, knowing from nature what the weather will be.

October holds no secrets or surprises for the farming countryside. The process of deep ploughing makes certain that all the undesirable weeds will be buried for another year and the land made clean.

Taking stock, the ploughman says what a delightful sight it is to see such perfectly deep straight furrows, pure satisfaction, all the walking miles, daily behind his faithful friend Stormer, his beloved horse, with one furrow plough.

His little girl enjoys the company, she is three or four or five years, not more, her little legs getting stronger making this journey each day. Something she insists on doing, her choice to meet her adored Daddy whom she admires immensely.

Living and being alongside all the beautiful animals on her farm, two other horses, Brandy, a mare, and an older boy, short, black with a white blaze on his nose, these two take turns at working, lots of other cart pulling, other types of machinery. Also there are generous cows who gave milk, and baby calves which she loves very much, to say nothing of the pigs and chickens.

A Special Day

Today for Polly has been more than the usual. This morning, in the house, Mummy and Granny are busy making food and cans of tea to take to the fields for Daddy and this is something she doesn't want to miss.

'We must get you into warm boots, and you certainly cannot go out into the cold air without warm clothes to protect you from getting cold.'

Ah! They're ready at last. Off goes Jack the dog, he's very fast and she can't keep up with him. By the time they're through the stackyard he's out of sight.

'No stopping him now,' she thinks to herself, 'I'll try running.'

'Don't go on too far ahead,' she hears Grandad shout.

The harvest has been successful this year; at least two stacks of wheat, two of barley, and others, there's five or six in the stackyard. It has been a nice dry summer and the crops have been safely gathered in with lots of hard work for horses and men alike, next comes threshing day fun.

Now, there's a little ditch at the end to get to the next field where the chickens are in big pens. There is a little bridge of two or three railway sleepers, quite worn, uneven, with a hole on the outside. As she hurries on to it, she slips, and the next thing is head first in the ditch, upside down, not in water, in vegetation, as soon the ditches will be cleared. Luckily Grandad comes along with the food parcels and drinks. The clever man has a weeding hook.

'Hold on there, my gal,' he says, hooking her out by the coat that she is wearing. Just a trivial unexpected delay, she is off again to reach the field, there she will remember to tell her dad what has happened. As with many similar events on the farm, his advice is,

'We won't tell Mummy and Granny, or they won't let you come along again.'

However, after this, Mummy would accompany her and Jack the dog to the field to share the ploughman's lunch, and enjoy the beautiful fresh air and the birds singing.

Wartime Childhood

It is 1941 when Polly is born. She will spend lots of time with her beloved granny with whom she has bonded almost at birth, as her mother has to remain in hospital for some weeks after her birth.

Granny is seventy years old, but a strong country farmer's wife who has always worked hard making butter to sell at the door. She has a lot of money saving ideas.

She feeds this adorable baby with a bottle. Daddy washes nappies and a cousin comes by to bathe baby Polly. This happens by the kitchen range.

The cousin has a six-month old baby of her own and lives in a pub with Polly's dad's older sister. Dad's sister had been married twice – and has had two silver weddings! At this time, the baby is in the pub with its granny.

The floor is covered in red pamments, cold and very hard. During one bath time, she drops baby Polly on the hard stone floor. Fortunately, no harm is done, and this is where Not Telling Mummy has its beginnings. Meanwhile, Mummy is still in hospital suffering through several operations. However, baby Polly is fine. Granny had worried that her old hands couldn't hold a wet baby whilst bathing her, but in hindsight it would have been better had she done it herself. Daddy takes Polly to the hospital to see Mummy, and all the nurses pass her around. Her mummy is quite ill with internal afflictions.

Months later, Mummy comes home from hospital, and normal family life continues. Life on the farm is good, lots of baby animals as each year passes. Mummy coming home was such a relief for Daddy, though he has coped with the help of his mother. Polly has bonded with Granny.

Snow Drifts

There is a very cold winter in 1947 with deep snow on the roads. Polly is six years old. There has been lots of snow, and with strong winds there are eight to ten foot drifts. The roads are impassable.

However, one of the parents from the next village is determined to take her small daughter to the private school in the town. She is driving in her small car along the road at the end of the farm drive which dips down some three or four feet.

She travels by this route each and every day, but in the snow is not anticipating the gradient in the road and she ploughs straight into the snowdrift. Polly's dad, the kind farmer, will help, of course he will, getting his tractor out and pulling her, her car and little daughter out.

She will not get to school today, though. These drifts to Polly are simply the first real snow she has ever seen, and there is so much ice on the ponds which are in every meadow. One of the rules every day is to break the ice wherever it may be on water tanks and ponds to enable the animals to drink, the hens also, the pigs, horses and cattle too, although lots of them try to eat snow.

Spring

Darling baby chicks, balls of yellow fluff, come in boxes of 50 or 100. Such a wonderful experience for baby Polly as she is allowed to take part in their wellbeing. They are in safe sheds attached to the farm house, with special warm lighted little houses where they are safe from the rats that are very interested in taking their food - or them. These homes are kept at a certain temperature as they act as incubators. These are day old chicks, just hatched from the eggs. They are not born at the farm, they arrive when they are a day old and have to be nursed to survive.

Time passes so quickly, in a week or two they will start to grow real feathers and soon be strong enough to come out onto the ground floor of their shed, run around and get strong legs. As dusk comes it is still very necessary to fasten all the sides of their little homes down to keep warmth in and rats out. Their little drinking and feeding troughs are so cute. Some chicks die, but very few, they are strong little cheep-cheeping creatures, far too many to name. Their purpose is to later on give daily, weekly or monthly cheques, once the eggs are sent to the Egg Marketing Board. Each box carries 30 dozen eggs and there are usually about six boxes. That's a lot of eggs.

This provides income so that farmers like Daddy are able to pay wages to the men who work on the farm, and also to keep little Polly, Mummy, Granny, and Grandad. This is only part of the income though; another source is the milk cheque which brings in more money as a regular income to enable the farming family to survive.

In these days of WWII, farming is a reserved occupation: the farmer is exempt from call up to war, as it is important to grow the crops for Britons to survive this terrible war while everyone is on rations.

This farm is about 100 acres, which means it is mixed farming with some cattle, milking cows, calves, pigs for bacon and pork, chickens for eggs and of course man's dear lifetime friend the horse. Across Britain, farming at this time is such, some are larger farms, of course, and some are small with only a few acres, these are small-holdings, of about fifteen to twenty-five acres.

Only the larger farms like Polly's are able to be self-sufficient, that means the wheat, barley, oats, peas, horse beans, potatoes, swedes and sugar beet can, when harvested, be sent to market and will realise monies to enable the farmer to obtain machinery to work the land for the forthcoming year. And so it is year on year, it is necessary to rotate the crops, to clear the root crops, and the soil is made free of all the weeds to stop the corn getting choked and dying.

Bicycle

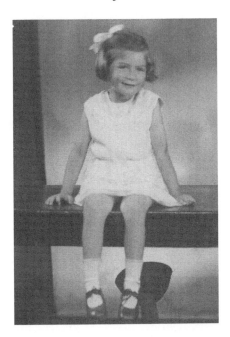

It is about the time Polly is three or four years of age and her Daddy has acquired a child's bicycle for her, but as it is war time there are no spare materials to buy to mend the bike. It is a fact that it needs some repairs; new tyres, seat and pedals at least, so there it is in a special shed by the farmhouse waiting safely until such time as she is old enough and the repairs completed. Until then it is impossible for her to ride as in these days there are no stabilisers for small children like her, of course she doesn't understand and it is clearly a fact that little Polly wants to see her bike and be sure that it is hers and hers alone.

'I want to see my bike,' she tells her mother and father repeatedly.

'You won't be able to ride on it, as it needs attention,' said Daddy.

Polly continues to insist that she wants to see her bike, and her parents eventually give in and take her to see it. She has waited so patiently to get a glimpse of her beloved bike, but when she sees it she just stands and looks at it, and says:

'I want a ride on that. I want a ride on that.'

And she continues to repeat this until the explaining is put across as best as can be explained.

As time passes and supplies become available, in due course, Polly's bicycle is ready for her to attempt to ride. Her loving mother and father stand a yard apart, walk her one to the other, who in turn pass her back. And so, day after day, she becomes more aware of balance and guidance as they venture further and further apart along the farm drive, with lots of large cobblestones, potholes and very rough ground.

She learns to ride her bike and after some weeks she can keep control and ride mostly safely, albeit on the farmyard surface. So now, after riding in a basket seat on the back of Daddy's bicycle, she has graduated to her own on the special journey of nearly three miles to Thelveton, where another grandmother lives close by an American air base. At the bottom of her garden, the GIs give Polly their candy and chewing gum. When she goes to talk to them they are so friendly to little sweet Polly, whose auntie worked on the base for them.

At her maternal grandmother's house, Polly strengthens her little legs cycling all that way. Ah, and as time passes by she is able to guide the bike herself whilst pedalling along the country lanes. Then when she is really strong and aware of how to control her bike, riding along between or in front of her parents.

One day, cycling along, Polly feels a horrible stinging pain in one of her eyes. The weather is warm, with lots of small flies about, and one has gone into her eye. She feels intense pain and starts to swerve all over the road, it is impossible to see as her eye begins to water, and both eyes are stinging with the hot pain. It is far too intense, and seeing her wobbling, her father shouts out to her,

'What are you doing? You will make your mother fall off her bike!'

It hasn't been long since Daddy had been holding her shoulder as she rode along, but until now, she has been able to manage to ride by herself for quite a long time. She is still very young though, four or five years old, not more, and of course the blue bicycle is so small.

Well, Daddy puts one hand to her shoulder as he has before when she rode on the roads the very first few times early on. The awful fly has to be washed out when they get to Grannie's house.

Polly cycles to Aunt Jessie, dad's sister, with milk every day and gets half a sausage when she arrives! Aunt Jessie is a businesswoman who sells goat's milk and cheese, and she is a very economical woman.

School

Time moves slowly whilst at school. In the infants' class everyone sits at desks for two, side by side, no talking! Her teacher is Miss Dowling. Polly is a pupil at Burston CP school, not the famous Strike School. It is a very strict school but a good one.

She is told off for talking, mostly. She simply can't be quiet.

The head teacher has a bun and looks very severe. Polly has a perm, and the teacher asks her, "Who's been bending your hair?"

At break time, a third of a pint of milk is given to each child, but Polly doesn't like the milk, especially in the winter when it has stood in front of the open coal fire and become warm. It is an even worse taste than when it is hot, so she swaps her bottle with the boy who is sharing her desk with her!

This boy has no fear. Later, Polly meets him at the plantation, which he walks to over the railway line. They love climbing.

They are no more than seven or eight years old.

Sometimes at infant school, the children are told to play with wooden bricks of various shapes and sizes, to build with them is a type of learning. Polly builds railways and towns and houses with long and square bricks, archways and flat pieces for roads.

Children are allowed to use paper and pencils at first to learn to write, and they also have some quite nice little story books, and things to help count.

For Polly, the very most awful thing is the knitting, it is horrid, strong wool, more like string, it hurts her hands when she is learning to knit, and gives her blisters.

Polly doesn't know yet that she will become a very clever knitter later in life, mostly because at home, Mummy helps her knit with much nicer wool.

Later on, she will win a competition in a woman's magazine for knitting a square, with perfect stitches and tension.

Singing, Concerts, and Sport

Polly thinks the best time at school is the oncoming of Christmas, with learning to sing songs, and having a part in the school plays. When Polly first goes to school, aged five, she sings Goodnight Mr Moon on the big stage, all by herself. She isn't nervous, she is a terrible show off.

The stage is at one end of a large classroom, made of boards on trestles. It's very strong, and safe for the children. The desks are pushed under the boards, and the chairs in rows like an auditorium. It's only a village school, but there are curtains up and someone to operate them, just like a real theatre.

Polly and the other children enter by the back door beyond which is the cloakroom and infant classroom where they change their costumes. This happens every year and one year Polly plays a Smart Lady and another year she sings A Partridge in a Pear Tree from The Twelve Days of Christmas. She has many leading roles, too many to remember. She always loves it.

When Polly is at school, she loves to sing in the school choir. Actually she is in several choirs, including her school one, the Burston Chapel Choir, the Diss Baptist Church choir, and the village school choir.

It is really such an experience, she loves so very much to sing. There is no need to practice especially, as her whole life is about singing. The High School choir is exciting. The headmistress is Miss Anita Jones, a Welsh singing teacher, who divides the choir into soprano, alto, mezzo soprano, and contralto, all the voices, and Polly has such a range that she can perform in all of them.

Polly also enjoys art, another favourite subject of hers. At the end of each year she wins the highly regarded art prize. From being a small girl Polly has all her drawings, paintings and sketches, everything to do with her art work, up on the wall for all to see and admire. The other children may be a tiny bit jealous.

When the Secondary Modern school opens, Polly is 14. She is a prefect straight away, and later head girl. Because she is an only child, she is good at communicating with adults. She has never been treated like a child by her parents, and so she isn't fazed by much. At this school, Polly dances in a Russian Wedding as the leading man of troupe of Cossacks, in wellington boots. This is really special and not ever to be forgotten, in front of an audience of a thousand people the school hall.

Polly enjoys playing tennis at High School, and netball too, which she has played since Primary. She loves swimming, and learns to swim at Blue Wave Swimming Pool in Diss.

Her father teaches her to shoot a 12-bore shotgun, which was always kept by the door, unloaded, of course.

Cattle, Bullocks, Heifers

As the mother cows have calves, the milk is sold as soon as the calves get stronger and it proves to be Polly's family's living wage.

Daddy feeds the calves milk as they are weaned. The females become heifers and the male calves are sold for beef. Once their teenage years come along, they will not be breeding bulls as that will need to be a special breed from another farm herd not related to any of these. They become bullocks once they have their parts removed. Females are heifers either if they do not calve, or after their first calf. Both kinds will hold reasonable part of the herd.

As they grow into teenagers, if you like, they are haltered up and led one by one into the meadow for grass. Until now they have mostly been inside the yard as they are very skittish and usually charging off in all directions. They really need to be monitored but also they are having special muscle-building food to become beef cattle. Once the babies are born, the heifers give perfect milk, and at the same time the bullocks go off to market for beef.

On one particular day, some of the village boys, Polly, and her father have six or eight heifers with halters around their necks when the farm dog comes home from visiting one of his bitches quite a distance away. Polly is directing the leading heifer, and her father is at the very back with the last one. The dog, Prince, comes to his master to report his home coming, something the heifers have never seen - a dog around the back of their ankles and feet – and it sends them into a stampede as Polly is holding their halters. Polly can hear her father calling.

'Hold on, hold onto the halters! Do not let go of your halter!'

Polly at the front is tumbled to the ground, onto the very hard stony walkway to the meadow. She is being dragged along by the heifer she is holding, and all the hooves, legs and feet of the other half dozen or so are banging against her head and body. Luckily, Polly isn't badly hurt, or hurt at all, it is a miracle. Needless to say after this, Daddy makes sure the dogs are at home and tied up at their kennels.

"Yes, another story not to tell mother," Polly thinks after she gets up and brushes herself down.

Polly and the Big Angry Bull

Little Polly is very happily playing in the farm yard with the dogs or watching the men working on various jobs around the farm yard building, when suddenly the peace is shattered by the sound of pounding hooves and snorting nostrils. Every so often the neighbour's bull visits Polly's family farm and Polly is alarmed, not knowing where to turn.

She scampers to the house to be with Mummy, and to feel safe inside her lovely home, absolutely scared stiff as this is the first time this has happened. As the years pass by, Polly realises that this happens often, especially when animals are calling to each other to do their duty.

The big bull is in fact being dutifully called to attend to the needs of a heifer that requires his services, for this is what nature intends. The bull is so ready and willing to do his services that he has nothing else in mind.

Of course, at the age of five or six, Polly is too young to understand what is happening, or the reason for the bull's intentions and why he is visiting her family's farm.

Quickly, the men put the bull away safely until his owner collects him.

The bull isn't particular about when he decides to escape and pay a visit to Polly's farm, or to anyone else in the village who has a needy cow. Sometimes the visits happen during the night, waking poor Polly up. It is terrifying. Everyone is rushing around trying to catch the big bull and put him in a pen until morning, but poor Polly is left traumatised for all her childhood.

In her adult life she has nightmares of the bull's visits and often wonders whether, if her parents had explained why the big bull visited, she may not be so frightened.

Of course the bull wasn't angry, just impatient, and the correct procedure for the services of the bull would be for the farmer to contact the cow's owner and make proper arrangements for such visits.

Baby Calves

As a result of all the visits from Mr Bull, Polly's farm has beautiful calves which will soon leave their mothers, having to be weaned off mother's milk. Polly will be able to help feed these babies by letting them suck her fingers covered in milk, cow's milk first, and gradually with small amounts of baby animal feed added to the milk mixture, just like weaning human babies. The calves will be sexed into male for beef, with the chop between their little back legs, and female for heifers and cows for breeding and milk.

Sometime in the 1940s in Polly's area a scientific breakthrough is first developed for use on farms. This is Artificial Insemination. Father would phone, and the AI would do the necessary, which would produce much better stock. Farmers could choose breeds, Friesians if you wanted good milkers for instance, they produced lots of quality milk and strong baby calves. For beef, Aberdeen Angus or Red Poll, and heifers for calves and milk.

However, Polly doesn't get to see any of this. She isn't allowed anywhere near this happening. So the cows lose their pleasures with the old bull who soon disappears. AI is the way forward.

Kicker

Kicker is a great milk-producer, and is hand-milked in the morning and evening, twice a day. Coming back from the meadow at the end of the day, she can hardly walk with her big udder so uncomfortably full of milk. At this time, she is around twenty-three or -four years old.

Before this time, earlier on in her years, Polly goes in winter evenings to sit in the nettice, or milking parlour. It is cosy there and she has enjoyed being there from the time she was small, young to be with her father. There is warmth from the animals, they give off a lot of body heat.

There could be eight or ten of them chained up at their own feeding mangers, each and every one has their own special feeding trough, they go straight to their own area where the food has been put for them, then father ties their necks up so in turn they can be milked.
All of them stand so beautifully still while they are milked, it is a relief to have the milk taken away. All of them except

35

Kicker, who is up against the wall at the end of the shed where a ring is secured in the wall. Here, she has her right back leg tied firmly to the wall to restrain her kicking whilst being milked.

Polly's father is the only one who milks her, he always says to Polly, "don't go near her at all, never", and so Polly stays well away from her and those powerful back legs.

This evening, the tilly lantern is hanging in place high, so it gives the best light from a high point. Suddenly without warning, the cow has an urge to kick as she is being milked. Before Polly realises what is happening, her father is kicked from his stool, and comes the length of the nettice, behind the backs of all the other cows.

This is the worst time ever, and Polly freezes, it all happens so quickly. Kicker has broken her restraining rope. Luckily Father has no bones broken, just some bad bruising, and quickly must find another strong rope to tie up that strong leg and finish the job of getting the milk from her.

There is no time to ponder over spilt milk as the milk in the pail has gone over. The three legged stool has gone as well, everything flying through the air. The other cows haven't flinched or moved, and all are calm. But father has to show Kicker that whatever she does to protest, she will never win. He ties her leg again and continues, it's for her health as well, being a source of earning profit.

More About Kicker

A few years after the milking parlour disaster, Kicker is impregnated by AI, as she is the best milk producer, up to a daily seven gallons. This is her 22nd calving.

As brave as he wants Polly to be, her father doesn't feel it's right for her to see new life emerging. Polly is 12 or 13, and always knows that Father knows best, and it isn't good for the animals to have a nervous person near them. She is always around, though, at these times, to be able to get on her trusty bike and go to the telephone box in the village when and if the vet is needed, and this is one of those times. Kicker has been in labour for several hours.

Polly isn't included in the actual birth, only the men do those things. Father calls to Polly to get the vet. There are six men trying to help to no avail. Taking the correct change for the red telephone box, she is at the phone within ten minutes. The vet's receptionist picks up at the other end. Polly says, "We need your help, please send a vet," then the receptionist says to her "get a rope and tie the feet," but Polly tells her "that is already happening, six men pulling, to no avail, and please come quickly."

Polly says earnestly she has to be certain that the vet will definitely arrive, this is a matter of life and death.

She is very confident that the person on the other end has understood. She cycles back as fast as her legs can push the pedals round. She reports back that it will be ten minutes, as the vet is in the next village.

Her father is really anxious. His workers are at hand and two friends from the village are also assisting. Things like this have never happened before, something is really wrong. The car arrives, and out gets the vet, putting his waterproofs on, apron, gloves and wellies. This is all Polly will see. He disappears into the shed where poor Kicker is having her baby.

After quite some time, when it is clear that all is over, the news comes: two baby black boy calves who have sadly died. Mother cow is very weak and poorly, she is good in spirits as she has been such a good addition to their herd. Polly's father will not allow her to be killed, she is a good friend and workmate, with a strong character, headstrong even, but she is much valued.

The sorry thing is that she is too weak to stand, never mind, with her determination she will recover fully, hopefully. The vet comes in every day to see if there is any progress, and it is necessary to turn her every day as otherwise she will get "bedsores" from lying in the same position. The village schoolchildren, boys who like to earn some money on the farm, come and see her progress. Nowhere like being able to stand up yet. There is a remedy for tired muscles which goes back a number of years, Polly's Granny, along with Father, think it might be possible to try this out on the patient.

Polly realizes that her dad and this excellent producer of milk have had many years together, a quarter of a century at least, with good times and not too many bad things, this episode is the worst.

The vet keeps visiting with advice. Kicker has healed inside with all the medication, and Polly uses the mustard bath, twice daily, on Kicker's tired weak muscles, mostly in her legs, and it is good to include her back also each day.

The vet tells everyone that "we must get her onto her feet." He demonstrates how to do this: jump noisily in her face, with a flash of white cloth or paper, something that is sudden, to alarm her. With this, she will be surprised and try to stand up.

Firstly, she will attempt to raise her head and front legs, the back legs won't budge an inch. To even be able to move her, from one side to the other, it requires many people, and it is done carefully with the help of some kind of sticks.

On this particular day as all were standing around, Polly's dad gave a big statement: "Now, all you boys, we know what to do, and it's time that she was on her feet. She's been like this for several weeks now we need her on her feet as her body has healed very well. We have to get her confidence back and strength in those legs front and back."

"What I will do, I'll give the first one to see her on her feet, that's all fours, half a crown from me," he says, very loudly and defiantly. Polly listens to that and understands all that is said.

As it is she who is giving the stimulation of the mustard bath, warm water and massage, and as she is always there by herself each day, she goes in and startles Kicker. Each time it happens the cow makes an effort to get up and it isn't long before she is almost standing. Polly continues to make a loud noise and motion that startles the cow into standing up. One day, that she comes up on all four feet and rocks only a little. Polly races off to tell her father with such excitement, she is so pleased.

"She's up! On her feet! I've done it! Just me!"

"Oh good," he says, "I'll come and see her," and he does. And each day now she becomes stronger, stays up longer, and is able to move slightly more each time.

But Polly doesn't get the half crown, and she doesn't ask. Her father intended it for the village boys. He starts bank accounts for some of them, for the money he pays them for jobs on the farm. They will be grateful when they are older, and will know how to save. He thinks Polly has enough money, and how would she spend it, anyway? He provides everything that she needs. Those boys will never have a half crown; he really would like them to have it.

However, it is Polly who has done all the nursing and hard work, bathing the injured cow with mustard baths, reviving the muscles, helping her heal both physically and mentally.

Birthday

On the day of Polly's eleventh birthday, her daddy goes off to town with lots of money in his back pocket. It is April 26th and lots of school friends are coming to Polly's birthday party. By three in the afternoon, friends started arriving.

The farm house is large enough, with lots of big rooms for everyone to run round, play games and have fun.

First they must sit down to the birthday tea prepared by Polly's mother who has been making cakes with lots of icing and sugar toppings. The sandwiches have egg and cress fillings, tuna and mayonnaise, ham and mustard, even jam sandwiches as those are Polly's favourite. There are cucumber sandwiches too. Then there are jellies, raspberry and orange flavours, also blancmange in the shape of a rabbit and round jellies like sandcastles made from other jelly moulds.

After tea, they go out to play in the farmyard, hide and seek and other games around the farm.

But who is this coming down the drive? It's Polly's daddy with her present, a large grown up bicycle. Called a Hopper, it's green in colour, and there is an identical one for her mother. Two identical green bicycles for his girls. Of course the one for Polly must be adjusted – handlebars right down low, and the same for the seat.

How excited they are with such a surprise! Polly can't wait to get on hers and go for a ride. This is the beginning of many miles on those wheels, with having to ride three miles to school and three back, and at weekends cycling a radius of twenty miles around the farm and villages for many years to come. Cycling is the finest form of transport that Polly has at this time. There are cars for some people, but not so many, and also motor cycles around the area, with its narrow roads which wind around leading to village after village.

Around the countryside are beautifully cut hedges with equally clean ditches with free running water that has drained from the fields via the mole draining that was customary in those times.

There is really no danger, or very little, unless the large bull comes pounding towards them down the road. Of course he needs to get to see his lady cow, he knows she's needing him.

Lady's
Model

Floods

It is 1953. Polly is 12 years old and outgrowing her clothes and shoes. The family hears of floods along the east coast, and there are collections of blankets, clothes, shoes and tins of food for the people affected, including over the channel in Holland. Many people are left with no homes or possessions.

Polly is so very fond of her shoes, which are in quite a new style. They are a special design that has never been seen before. Polly has only worn them once, she hasn't properly grown out of them, and oh, she really has fallen in love with them. But off they go to Holland for people who had lost everything. They are not worn at all, this is something she will never forget. It seems that Polly's mother has given everything away, she has nothing left. At this time, she is growing very fast.

Girls – Girls – Girls

We should know that as Polly is growing up, she has such happy times with her mother and grandmother, who she affectionately calls Granny. Her mother, who is Ida Ellenor, when shopping for clothes for Polly, purchases the really good quality items. There is a special shop in Diss that she always uses.

Polly loves especially two little dresses that she has when she is three or four years old that are blue velvet, one is dark blue and the other light blue, so pretty with smocking across the front panels and bright stitching which gives a beautiful finish. Always when wearing her special dresses, Mother changes them so they keep fresh and crisp.

Sometimes they go to the great big city, Norwich, which has wonderful shops and things to see. Ida likes Norwich, and worked there before she married and came to the farm; now they go to the city by catching the train at Burston Station, where they live. The farm fields adjoin the railway line from Norwich to London Liverpool Street station.

Polly loves the train, the ride is so exciting, looking out of the windows, sometimes scenes of frost, snow and ice, in fact almost a whiteout. There's the occasional cock pheasant in the field with his beautiful striking colours, red head, black and brown feathers, the beautiful male bird. The female is much more discreet, her colours blend in with the scenery, because she has a brood of eggs she is attending and soon the babies will hatch. She needs to stay safe, her time looking after her young is precious, and she could have up to fifteen babies.

This is Polly's favourite wild game bird, as at a special time, in the season, they are shot and ready for roasting for the table, a most delicious food if prepared and cooked correctly, and served with ideal accompaniments.

These lovely birds are protected by law, as are many other game birds and animals in the countryside.

After six or eight stops at stations, they reach the very big station at Norwich City. The journey from the station to the shops is by bus.

One time, during the weeks before Christmas, Polly's daddy comes along. They arrive at a large shop with toys on one floor above the elevator. They come upon a pyramid of dolls and on the very top is a bride doll. Polly isn't interested in that. She has seen a black boy doll dressed in sailor uniform complete with a sailors' hat. It's lower down in the display, much nearer the floor.

Daddy and Mummy would like Polly to choose the bride doll but no, she is adamant she is to have the sailor boy doll. It is so unusual, she has never ever seen one before. However much they try to persuade her, she won't change her mind. She keeps the doll for years, and plays with him always, he has a special place in her heart. This is only the second doll she's ever had. Granny gave her a baby doll one Christmas, but she has never had a pram or a tea set.

One day, when she is eight or ten, Polly is visiting with a friend who lives on another farm near her uncle's and in the playroom there is a tea set. Polly thinks it is beautiful. It is metal, with a pretty painted design on it. Polly never ever forgets that lovely tea set but never gets one herself.

Another time, when Polly is very young, her mother and an aunt take her to Ipswich, which is in the direction of London, by train. Polly is so tired this day her mother has to carry her after shopping, as there has been a lot of walking. Mummy purchases a push-along horse that Polly can ride on. She loves him and keeps him for years, she calls him Deppar. He has a handle so that she can push him when there is no-one to push her outside. He helps her learn to walk.

An uncle makes her a doll's house with furniture, it's practical, not glamourous but she enjoys it.

Polly doesn't have too many toys; she likes reading books and writing books and colouring books. In the local newspaper there is a children's column called Aunt Jane's. Polly joins this club and enters many competitions. One week she is featured in the storyline column.

One time the competition is for a drawing or painting of a landscape. Polly produces a farm scene with a large collie dog and distant fields and meadows beyond the farmyard buildings. This of course wins first prize out of all the very many entries.

Bridge Green Farm Girl

For the Youngsters
by AUNT JANE

Dear Children,

First of all I have some bad news for you, that stalking winter-demon, 'Flu, has stung Aunt Jane at last. She is now in bed and can do no more than send love to you all. As Uncle Jeff and Cousin Dick are very busy, I shall try my best to deal with your letters and competitions this week.

First let me introduce myself to you:

Aunt Jane has got the 'flu —
And I am Cousin Sue
Who has had it too;
And Cousin Dick
Was also sick
O what a tale of woe
Of mumps and colds and snow!

Aunt Jane told me what a large number of new members there were, and I, yet, this morning, counted another twenty new applications. I didn't realise what a lot of children there were in Diss and the district around.

This week's new members are: Montague Norman, Cross Street, Eye (7); Brenda Smith, 2 Council Houses, Tivetshall (5); Pat Rumble, 2 Mere Street, Diss (7); Gillian Kitchen, 34 Uplands Way, Diss (9); Pat Ruby Lee, "Wood Cottage," Beeston, St. Andrew, Norwich (8); Brenda May Lee, "Wood Cottage," Beeston, St. Andrew, Norwich (5); Rita Jean Lee, "Wood Cottage," Beeston, St. Andrew, Norwich (6); June Ford, Bridge Green Farm, Burston (9); Christine Chamberlain, 20 Eaton Road, Sidcup, Kent (6); Diane Chamberlain, 20 Eaton Road, Sidcup, Kent (6); (Christine and Diane are twins); Ann Draper, The Dale, Thorpe Abbotts, Diss (8); Ian Scotland, 16 Castle Crescent, Wingfield (7); Roland Copping, Church Street, Stradbroke (11); Margaret Lockwood, "Normandale," Dickleburgh (7); Maureen Ann Lummis, "Ark Villa, Thornham Parva (4); Maureen Howard, Union Lane, Weyb, ham (11); Maurice Watson, Heckfield Green, Hoxne (12); Charles William Vincent, Brook Cottage, Fressingfield (8); Robert Draper, "Normandale," Dickleburgh (7); Gwen West, 29 Mill Road, Thorpe Abbotts, Diss (9).

It seems that most of you want a few days in bed with your dolls and its around you and tasty meals brought up on a tray by Mummy. And bed is a lovely place in this cold weather, don't you agree? though it's not much fun to have aches and pains and big swollen necks — so, I hope that those of you, who have to snuggle under your sheets, will soon be up and about again.

There were quite a number of newsy letters addressed to Aunt Jane and I expect you will be interested to know what some of the members of the Children's Corner have to say. Maureen Howard, one of the new members, tells us that she has three cats to whom she has given the lovely names of Mossy, Tabby and Fluffy. I wonder if they are all brother and sister cats? She is a member of "Our Dumb Friends' League" and is very fond of animals. Maureen has sent in a useful suggestion for a competition and I am sure that Aunt Jane will make use of it later in the year. Montague Norman, who has just joined the Children's Corner, tells us that he goes to the Eye National School and also belongs to the Cubs. I expect he has a lot of friends and a good deal of fun at Cubs. He, with the help of his sister, has just made a badge. I wonder what the badge is for? It is quite a good idea to make a badge yourselves, to show that you are members of the Children's Corner. Perhaps you could all send in some suggestions of how to make badges, and what to put on them. It should be quite easy and rather fun.

Another interesting letter was one from June Ford, who attends the Burston Primary School and tells me that half of the pupils have been away with 'Flu and colds; June was one of the absentees herself. I hope, however, that she will be able to join the party which is going to the pantomime, on Thursday, to see "Mother Goose."

June seems to have a busy time, making herself very useful on the farm, helping to milk the cows and even driving her father's tractors. June has some lovable pets, a Collie called Prince and a Spaniel called Lassie, a large cat and even a horse with the suggestive name Stormy. Last summer she had her photograph taken, sitting on Stormy. Do you look after your pets yourself?

Let me thank you all for your letters on behalf of Aunt Jane. I shall see, that she gets them, when she is better.

PRIZEWINNERS

And now for the competitions! Well, it was far easier to judge this week's than last week's competition, when we were all pronouncing and mispronouncing and arguing over your word-couples, which poured in in hundreds!

The senior competition: an account of a visit to the pantomime, brought in many colourful descriptions. It made very interesting reading for me, as I was unable to visit a pantomime myself this year, and luckily most of you had been to different ones, "Mother Goose," "Cinderella," "Dick Whittington," "Jack and the Beanstalk" and "Little Red Riding Hood."

I have awarded the prize to Rita Crowe (12) after a great deal of consideration, because there were many good entries, particularly that of Christine Watson (10), who wrote a lively and chatty account of "Cinderella." But Rita Crowe gave a smooth description of the outing, including little incidents which occurred by the way, thus making the reading of her composition very entertaining.

However, I must also congratulate Pamela Rout (11), Margaret Watson (13) and Brenda Lanham (10) for their very good entries.

The juniors too submitted very colourful and imaginative drawings of a pantomime scene, which they had seen. The prize goes to Barbara Newman of Stradbroke, who sent in a very good drawing of a scene from "Mother Goose," although she is only five. But Barbara Holmes (7), Rosemary Flatman (9), Zillah Mary Baker (6) and Christine Watts (5) deserve mention for their imaginative entries.

HAPPY BIRTHDAY

Many happy returns to all those whose birthday falls this week! I am sorry I can't mention your names individually, but I can't find Aunt Jane's big birthday book. However, we shall make up for it next time. In the meantime, have an enjoyable day!

London

Granny and Aunt Jessie travel a lot each summer, and sometimes visit an aunt and uncle in London. This involves a train journey then a taxi to Blackheath SE3. Polly loves the train and when she's seven or eight she's invited to go along for the summer holidays with Granny and Aunt Jessie. It is such an exciting journey, she loves it so much, she is never afraid or apprehensive as she trusts her beloved Granny so much. Polly is left in London while Granny and Aunt Jessie travel to a seaside resort on the south coast.

Polly stays with her Auntie Mary in Blackheath in a medium sized flat in a large town house with bay windows, consisting of three or four flats. In the house next door, Polly makes friends with a little German girl named Ota Weitmann. They play most days in the garden, and Polly enjoys this friendship very much, looking forward to her games of five stones, skipping, ball games and hide and seek.

On other days they go shopping. Auntie Mary belongs to the Townswomen's

Guild. Polly goes along with her and sits very quiet and still as it's a ladies' meeting. Every so often the underground train comes along, it makes such a noise and shakes the room. The line runs underneath the building and everyone stops talking until the train passes. Polly finds this amazing but doesn't get any explanation. Aunt Mary and everyone else in the room are accustomed to this happening. It's certainly such a different life and goings on from back home in the country on the farm!

Each year as the time passes, in the holidays Polly enjoys these breaks in London with Auntie Mary. Auntie Mary would say

"It's Saturday! Children's Cinema at Greenwich Odeon, or play in the park on all the children's apparatus?"

Although Polly is now nine or ten years old she is quite nervous about going along by herself to meet other children. However, it is quite a change from being in the country on the farm with maybe just one or two children, to a cinema full of noisy Londoners who possibly were all from the same school.

One day Polly has been out with her Auntie Mary and arriving home she can hear voices. When she enters the room, her two cousins Derek and Dennis are in the depths of something extraordinary. It becomes clear that one of them is inside one of the two wardrobes. Polly thinks he has been locked in by the older brother, she feels anxious. She asks:

"Why is he inside? What are you doing to him? Poor little boy, let him out!"

She is almost beside herself and she pleads,

"Let him out of there, in the dark all by himself."

These two 'boys' are in their early twenties, and happily developing black and white photographs. Colour photography is still uncommon in home developing. They are so amused by Polly and her worries.

On top of the wardrobes are large model aircraft which they have each built, and take to the Heath to fly with a remote control. These are so big that the fuselages hang over each end of the wardrobes, and the wings underneath are to be assembled on arrival at the heath. These occasions are something unknown to Polly and she is so impressed it is unimaginable.

Polly loves the London trams, the banging and bumping, shaking and noise, in contrast to the trolley buses that have just been introduced, on the rubber wheels which make her feel nauseous, very unwell. She loves the trains and trams that all run on metal and not rubber tyres.

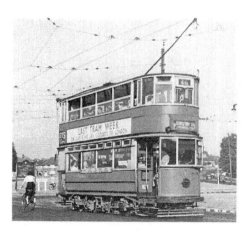

Back home, her Aunt Jessie's big Austin car really makes her feel very poorly with the different smells of Aunt Jessie's and Granny's fur coats, and the petrol fumes and the combination of them all.

Polly loves coming to London each year in the summer school holidays to stay the whole six weeks, so looking forward to the different way of life and a change of scene. She loves walking along the Docklands path by the Thames on Sundays with Auntie, and Uncle who stops in the olde worlde pubs in Woolwich, Greenwich, Lewisham, and Blackheath. Over on the ferry, or under the tunnel, Blackwall Tunnel, Woolwich ferry.

It is such an education for Polly, the little farm girl, to be with her aunt in the great capital of her country; leaving back home her mother and father to mind the farm. It is a very busy time for harvest and her mother will have to make food and cans of tea to take to the field where the corn is being cut, no time to come home or stop for dinner in the day, the meal has to be taken to the fields. Just as in winter and autumn when ploughing, in this case her mother will have baked a large meat and potato pie, possibly the previous day, and the men will all have a portion with a cup of tea. There's not much time to rest, maybe they will stop for fifteen or twenty minutes.

Polly continues to stay with her Aunt Mary in London each summer holiday, getting to understand the hustle and bustle of the city suburbs, seeing the demise of the handsome old trams which she loves. Until one fateful early spring, it is May or June, when the dreadful news arrives that her precious aunt has died - so sad is Polly, not being able to go on her annual visit.

However, two years later, friends who lived in Hampstead beside the Heath invite Polly to go and visit with them. She is now fifteen years old and has quite a different outlook on things.

With the house backing onto Hampstead Heath, she takes the friend's dog to get some exercise on the Heath, these friends have older daughters who are all out working in the city of Westminster. The parents work in the Houses of Parliament. She just stays for maybe two weeks this one year. They take her to see the London sights. But she misses her precious auntie. This auntie has, incidentally, been one of the earlier original midwives of Poplar and Greenwich. Such a widely respected lady, and much loved by the community.

Family Ties

At one time, Polly's Uncle Dick had a detached retina. She must have only been seven or eight, and was staying with Aunt Hilda while she was going up to the hospital to see him. Her mother, Mahalia, lived with them. While Polly was staying there, Mahalia died, but Polly took that very much in her stride. She didn't panic or scream or react badly. She was tough and independent, because of her upbringing on the farm, and the attitude of her suffragette grandmothers.

Mother and Home Loving

While Polly is very young and delicate, inside the farmhouse her mother keeps things clean, tidy and warm, always having to cook each and every day big hot meals. She has no time to do any work in the outside farm life, she is far too busy with the many jobs that happen inside.

One of these is to clean and buff the fifteen to twenty dozen eggs that are collected each evening from the free range hens and brought in; this is a late evening job after tea. Every week Polly's mother and father send from the farm between six and ten wooden boxes of thirty dozen eggs. When Polly grows old enough, she will help clean the eggs and put them carefully into trays of thirty.

In the Kitchen

First thing each morning the kitchen range fire needs to be lit. This is a black grate that is in the centre of the outside wall, as the chimney is in the centre, on one side of the grate is an oven which is used for baking. On top of this are round plates which can be lifted to enable saucepans of vegetables and such like to heat on top, and of course the kettle for tea and coffee.

In the right hand corner of that wall is a copper, which mother fills with water and which has another grate beneath it, so a fire is lit to boil the beautiful white sheets and nappies and towels, any item that is made of white linen or cotton. Also, at the very last, father's milking coats and aprons which are boiled. The most delicate go in first, and the things more discoloured follow once the previous lot is taken out. Then these have to be rinsed so many times in big baths that stand outside, and wrung with a very strong mangle. It has two large wooden rollers and mother feeds the wet clothes through by turning a wheel which has a handle on the side to make it work, and this crushes most of the water out.

In the left corner of the wall is a Dutch Oven which has a grate for fire underneath but unlike the copper it is never used, and hasn't been since Polly was born.

There is a shallow long sink along the other outside wall and above this is a very high shelf, which the wireless stands on. The wireless works with accumulators which have to be recharged each week. They are collected by the wireless shop owners who recharge them with a liquid acid, and are similar to a car battery but much smaller. They are made of very thick glass, about nine inches tall, and three by three square with a strong metal handle.

Listen with Mother, The Archers, and music on the wireless, which Polly and her mother love, but in the evening sometimes father listens to Sonny Liston and other heavyweight fighters.

The wireless is good for listening to the King's or Queen's messages and sometimes the Prime Minister makes an announcement, as in 1945 when the Second World War ended.

The television

When the BBC television signal is projected into our area, father thinks it might be an incentive to purchase a television set, something to please the village urchins who come to earn small amounts of money by doing the farm jobs that they can be trusted with.

While Polly, now nearly a teenager, is helping her mother with the eggs, the men and boys are watching football on the black and white television. They have, out of decency, removed their muddy boots and left them by the front door in the hallway. Polly and her mother don't want to venture to the room where all those smelly feet are. Once the news gets around that the family have a television, many more want to come, until the sitting room is standing room only.

The farmhouse chimney

Incidentally, the chimney has wide steps going up the inside to the highest point where the small boys were able to scrape the soot that cakes on hard. This was the intention because when the sweep put up brushes and his scraping tools, the area was so wide these hardly touched the sides. This is the method used in previous centuries with young boys, which was very efficient. In Polly's time, this doesn't happen. The farmhouse is five hundred or so years old and many such stairs remain hidden away, and suddenly come to light when least expected. There will always be the unusual found in a very old house when least expecting it, like a built-in time capsule.

Goodbye Grandad

Polly's Grandad has been in hospital to have an abdominal operation which involves him having a colostomy bag. Granny has to clean and dress his wounds. Polly doesn't know anything about this at the time.

It's 1947 and this year sees the departing of dear Grandad. He dies in the large lounge in which he has been sleeping for some months as he has been bedridden. Granny has the lounge looking beautiful with ornaments, clocks and pictures, a piano, a nice chaise-longue and some Queen Anne chairs. The room is nearly thirty feet square, it is a very large space. The clock on the mantelpiece stops at the time of his dying.

At this time the undertaker brings a coffin, and puts Polly's grandfather inside, washed and dressed in his best suit. The body remains in the coffin in the lounge where the curtains are drawn, also the neighbours close their curtains as a matter of respect until the day of the funeral when family and friends come to the house and give their goodbyes.

One of these mornings, Polly asks her granny, "Why is my grandad lying in there?" to which Granny replies, "It's his last little bungalow," as he had always said he would buy a bungalow. Granny picks up Polly so that she can kiss her grandad goodbye.

On the day of the funeral the undertaker comes and screws the lid of the coffin down and everyone follows on behind the hearse. Sometimes drawn by horses, or in this case by a smart car, it was a stately occasion. Polly doesn't really quite understand but she realises that she will never see her grandad again.

The double plot at the cemetery is booked and paid for and now awaiting the death of grandma. Grandma shows Polly where all the clean white clothes and everything are in the special drawer in the huge chiffonier. Grandma wants Polly to be sure to remember so that she can explain to the undertaker as to what her dear granny needs to be dressed in for the very last time. Polly is about six years old at this time but she will always remember. Granny thinks that by the time she goes, Polly will be old enough to help with the arrangements. It will not be for many years to come, as granny reaches the age of ninety before her passing, another sixteen years yet.

Women's Work

Living on the farm continues very much the same, Polly's mother still has a ration books for the clothes but doesn't need one for food so much as the farm provides most things. Granny makes butter with two churns at once, standing between them and turning both handles until the butter becomes set. She will carry on all night if need be, constantly turning, turning, and the butter she will also sell at the door and also makes home-made bread, pork cheese, yoghurt, and sourmilk cheese, so very many delicious foods.

Polly's mother is kept busy baking meat pies, meat and vegetable pies, fruit pies, apple and plum, as there is an orchard with many apple, pear and plum trees, and a huge walnut tree.

Some of the younger men and boys who work on the farm have no mother at home therefore they are in need of a nutritious meal for their strength and endurance as farm work is very strenuous and they need much energy, so it is necessary for them to have food with the family.

Every day Polly's mother makes a hot midday meal with meat and vegetables. Mother works very hard with all that cooking. At the end of the season when all the fruit has ripened there will be much more than needed for daily meals. This is the time to preserve the mass of fruit that is gathered. Mother gently cooks the fruit, boils it and puts into Kilner preserving jars that have an airtight rubber seal on the lid. It might be pears, or plums or other fruit, or the walnuts that fall from the trees before properly formed are pickled. Also, when there is a surplus of green tomatoes they get made into chutney with apples and sultanas.

Absolutely nothing is wasted, there is a huge storeroom next to the kitchen where all these preserves, fruits, jams, pickled walnuts, pickled onions, pickled beetroot and chutneys will go. All around the walls are shelves that are well fitted and strong to take all these many bottles and jars. There is also a spare room where the good picked apples are stored through the winter, when they are stored correctly with air circulating they won't go rotten.

There is one apple, the Blenheim Orange, that can always be relied upon to stay fresh through winter, and which tastes beautiful both straight off the tree and also good when stored, it's very special, this apple.

A Farmer's Wife's Work is Never Done

If this isn't enough for Polly's mother to do, sometime during the week, or even at the weekend she bakes lots of cake, shortcake, farm cakes, buns, sausage rolls and lots more besides; this is every week without fail. These cakes and such are offered by Polly's father to the strong contingent of lorry drivers who come to collect the milk and eggs, to deliver the animal feed, representatives from companies too many to mention.

"Come in and have a coffee, would you like a sausage roll or mince pie?"

Perhaps then they have a discussion around the kitchen table. And these are not mini-cakes!

When her mother makes the hot meals, Polly loves the way the potato is mashed as eggs and milk are plentiful. In go two eggs, with the bright orange yolks, and milk, and some butter to give the potatoes a creamy nutritious feel about them, this mixture gives them a very tasty feel, and a tiny pinch of salt and pepper. Another thing that mother does when cooking Yorkshire puddings, she adds suet to give a spongey effect, they are gorgeous also.

Then when the meals, cooking and everything else are finished, the water has to be brought in and put into large saucepans to boil on the stove as there are no hot or cold water taps. They use clean rain water which is collected in a large five-hundred-gallon tank outside the kitchen door. The tank is covered by a felt and wood top, the downpipe from the guttering is covered at the bottom with a strong sock or stocking tied on very tight, which catches any pieces of moss from the roof tiles. The water is beautifully soft, very clean and used for everything except drinking. The drinking water is taken each and every day from the hundred-foot well. This had the most beautiful taste.

There are people from six other homes using Polly's well for water, each in turn they come and collect it every day. No one has to pay.

Prisoners of War Working in the Fields

One summer's day when Polly is still really small, not yet at school, there is a lot of noise outside the kitchen door. Close beside her mother, Polly is intrigued to investigate. Her father is standing against the well, whilst in the yard, there are twenty or more men speaking a different language. Polly can't understand them, they have a strange way of speaking.

Father says to mother, "Keep hold of her, keep her in the house."

These men are Italian prisoners of war. They have come from their camp at Botesdale to work in the fields and are all wanting water as they have had nothing to drink or eat. But they don't get invited in for any of mother's cakes.

Gangs of these Italians are transported daily to farms to help with certain tasks such as harvesting, all work that is done by hand. They are brought in lorries, ten or twelve in a gang, with a guard.

It may be Germans another day, just a lorry load turns up with little warning to see if they can be of any help to the farmers, as many young men have left for war. Polly's father is needed for the work on the farm so he doesn't have to join the men who have gone off to war.

Many of the farms have ladies from the big cities and towns come to work on the land and they are called Land Girls. There isn't a need for them to work on Polly's farm as her father's tractor driver is not considered fit enough to go to war, and the younger men are not strong or healthy enough, so it is that uncles and other relations that live locally come and help when needed.

Many local people are known to Polly's family which is helpful all around, they can come and earn extra money chopping out sugar-beet, cattle beet and mangel wurzels, and weed in the early months of growth with a hoe, it is called 'singling' whilst the plants are very young and small and gives them reasonable space in between for the best to grow. In winter they are huge, and with snow and frost on the ground, the men, together with father take one in each hand by the green tops and bang them together to get the soil off, which is mostly clay, this is extremely hard and heavy work as the beet grow so very large.

The men need to tie a hessian sack around the front of them from the waist to below their knees because of all the wet, muddy clay soil which needs to be removed from the sugar beet. They lay the beet piles along the rows which are in turn collected and loaded onto a tractor and trailer, or indeed the horses Stormer, Brandy and Short, will pull a tumbril, which is a kind of small farm cart, and then in turn are taken to the railway station where they are loaded onto rolling stock trucks with each farmer's name marked on the wagon. When they arrive at the factory, each is assessed for size, weight, quality and cleanliness. This is very important as the payment is dependent on condition. Rarely does any prisoner of war help with this as it is too cold for them.

This is another way that Polly's father makes an income, the harvesting of the sugar beet. This is the way that agriculture is run in those years of the

1940s and 1950s. There were a few modern instruments like tractors, but mostly it is still manpower, together with horse power.

Polly grows up amongst mixed farming, growing crops, beef cattle, milking cows, chickens, laying hens, eggs, corn, barley for beer, wheat for cereals, oats for porridge, peas and beans, horsebeans for the horses' feed, clover for hay for the horses. It has such a beautiful aroma, does the clover, when cut and stacked into hay mounds, and

Polly's father has the largest knife to cut squares of hay in huge lumps for the horses to indulge. This knife has a blade the size of a small man's body with a giant handle. To cut the hay, it has to be pushed down, moved along, down again, until a generous square is shaped for the large, heavy horses. This is their evening treat after a hard day at work in winter.

In summer, after a hard day, they come back to the farmyard and have a long drink. The farmer is supposed to count their swallows as it is dangerous to have too many. Then they are safe, a halter put on their necks and led to their special meadow, where once inside the gate their halters are slipped off their necks. Polly watches as they kick up their back legs and gallop to the back of the fifteen-acre meadow which they have all to themselves from four o'clock or so until dark at ten or after. It is their finest hour; they thoroughly enjoy themselves after a hard day in the hot summer sun pulling the farming implements or the hay wagons.

It is wonderful to see them so happy enjoying the large open space and each other's company, and they are completely safe.

Fir Tree Plantation

It is October, and the horses are enjoying the long evenings. At the very end of the meadow, there is a large plantation of fir trees, and alongside the trees, large mushrooms suddenly appear. Polly goes along with her mother to pick these mushrooms. Each day, more will have grown. Polly has a small basket as she likes to be able to take some herself. They are lovely, very white on top and underneath like black velvet and they are so very tasty to eat.

No one ever becomes ill after eating these mushrooms which grow so huge; they last just a few weeks, and the family enjoy them. Polly thinks it's thanks to the horses that they grow so big.

Beyond the plantation there is an area of wet ground that doesn't ever dry up. It's not a ditch or a pond or pool or any of these types of water. But one time after Polly had been climbing the tall seventy or eighty foot trees that would sway, and once at the top would bend over, she was there in secret as the boy she used to share her milk with lived on the other side four or five fields over to the east. He asks her to meet him there and together they find a tall strong fir tree and climb to the very top. They make the top swing and sway. They are still quite young, and fearless. Her friend persuades her to meet him, maybe they were ten or eleven years old.

The truth is that Polly doesn't tell her parents where she is going as it is this land on the far side that is always damp, and one of them accidentally stands on it once, and it begins to pull them down. Luckily they are not heavy, so jump aside and save a dangerous outcome. This ground can suck a very heavy person or animal down and it really is out of bounds. It's part of the reason that the small wooded area is planted, and it also serves as a windbreak across the landscape of fields against the north east winds because it would have been very exposed without it.

Shopping with Granny in Norwich

Granny's eyes are not so good now cataracts were forming. She loves and adores her little granddaughter, and it is time to do some clothes shopping. As she spent lots of time with little Polly, she needs her to come along to tell her the prices of things. Granny tells Polly "You are my eyes, you help me to see and understand the labels."

One day, off they go to the train. Polly loves train journeys. "We will be in Norwich in half an hour," granny tells her. This is very rewarding. All the very big shops are in the large city of Norwich. Great shops with moving stairs (escalators), such excitement. They go into many; then it's lunchtime, all the way up to the fourth floor to the restaurant. The plate of food that arrives for Polly is really special, potatoes that are in a perfect ball, small pieces of everything on small plates, arranged to show the surface of the plates beneath, such an enjoyable event, being with granny by herself to explore all of the city's shops, and to eat in the big city. She doesn't have the chance to do this with mother. However, they must catch the afternoon train now for home and tea. Granny is pleased with her achievements, and with Polly's help.

They enjoy the pleasant train ride home, setting sun behind the trees, small rivulets and wild birds settling to their nests with food for their babies. The proud pheasant, who stands, looking everywhere for a challenge he is so special. Further along by a bend in small stream stands a proud swan admiring his pen and cygnets as they take to the water, for the first time maybe. A bright, mostly blue, kingfisher waits on a branch by the water hoping for a small fish for his young brood in the nest. Small areas of mist form as the chill of the day descends and darkness is falling.

When they reach the station there is a twenty-minute walk home. Polly can see the farm house from the railway but is sadly not able to take a short cut across the fields in her smart city shoes and clothes. Granny is her seventies now and can't cross the ploughed fields and headlands, which are the grass edges around the fields, and she certainly won't want to jump the ditches. However, they are soon home after a well spent day. It was another learning curve for Polly, with lots to tell mum and dad this evening.

Health and Doctors

Life on the farm for everyone is generally happy with no quarrels and little sickness, apart from Polly, who comes from school with those children's complaints which she manages to catch. First measles, then whooping cough, mumps and the dreaded chicken pox, all of which her mum and dad catch too, as when they were small children those ailments weren't around so much. Polly has awful colds with horrendous earaches. When she is too ill and feverish to get out of her bed, she sometimes has such a high temperature that it makes her hallucinate, suffering so very badly with her ears. Mother puts a large piece of cotton wool on her ear, soaked in methylated spirit, to cool her pain. This is tied on with large white handkerchief around her head. It somehow seems to soothe it.

Any illness that occurs, the doctor is sent for, he will arrive the same day, on his rounds. He will assess the severity of the illness or pain, and give some advice, write a prescription that can be picked up from his dispensary, and he will call again in two or three days' time.

This is after 1948 when Aneurin Bevan has introduced the National Health Service. Nye Bevan is a Labour parliamentarian from Wales. Having the NHS means that all health matters are free at the point of need, and paid for by taxes. It is a wonderful thing, after so many years of having to pay for a doctor, and not always having the money.

There are excellent doctors for Polly and her family, wonderful doctors and services and medicines. They don't need, they never have call for, hospitals much, as the nearest one is Norwich which is thirty miles away.

However, small ailments don't really affect anyone, as the grown-ups are able to keep well by eating well and living healthily. All foods, the weekly joint of meat and such, are kept in the cold dairy in a meatsafe, which has metal sides and front. The metal has small holes in it to allow the air through, but not flies, or small creatures. Polly's mum's is large, with two huge shelves in the space. It's about four feet wide, and thirty inches high, and about eighteen inches deep.

This is ample space for all the perishable foods. The dairy is a room that faces north, with lots of air vents and marble top shelves, and it is the coldest room in the house.

The womenfolk are expert at keeping food safe to eat, which is why a meat safe is called that - because it keeps food safe. Seldom or rarely does anyone have stomach trouble through bad food, that just doesn't happen as the house is always cold with draughts coming through the doors and windows. There are only coal fires and the occasional paraffin heater, and none of them are anywhere near the dairy or meat safe.

Mothers teach daughters how to keep and manage food, and everything that is necessary for staying out of harm's way with illnesses. It is extremely important that the girls are taught how to cook, bake and respect the handling of raw meat, fish and all perishable foods, even vegetables.

Polly is a poor eater; she is not interested in the good foods on the farm. When she was younger, her mother would cut a small sliver of Mars Bar a day for her daughter, hoping she wouldn't be ill with that much sweet richness of toffee and chocolate. It just isn't done to eat large amounts of confectionery. The doctor once told Polly's mum that her little daughter would never be fat. Mother is very concerned that Polly won't eat her meals and doesn't seem to enjoy all the good fresh food that is painstakingly prepared for her.

Kitchens don't have any worktops or cupboards around the room. All the food preparation is done on the kitchen table on wooden chopping boards. When Polly is eleven years old in 1955, mains water is laid on. Until then, hard water is from taken from the well just outside the kitchen door. To cook and bake, fires need to be lit and coal and wood has to be available to make ovens and grates ready for large amounts of food. Polly's family won't have electricity installed until she is fourteen years of age in 1958.

Such a transition then, running water on tap and lights every time you touch a button on the wall. Father and mother make sure that they fully understand this new modernization in the home; how much does it cost? We are all looking at the manuals that explain how many hours a 100-watt bulb will burn for – 10 hours for a penny, in old pounds, shillings and pence. The electric fire in the lounge has one bar, and runs for one hour for a shilling. There is a second bar, but the heat isn't the same as a coal fire, not as cosy somehow.

In the kitchen, space was made for a GEC electric cooker. Mother studied the manual again with its advisory recipes and times for cooking and temperature guides. For Polly and her family, it all seemed very posh; somehow though, the food didn't taste so nice, more dried up. Not such moist cakes and pies, but also not so much preparing and cleaning fireplaces and oil lamps that adorned the tables, the odd candle here and there and tilly lanterns that had to be hanging and carried to the milking parlour.

More extraordinary still, there is no inside toilet and bathroom. The outside toilet is out of the back door down a smooth path, five yards to a little door where inside is a mahogany bench seat with the same wooden cover, the smartest toilet for that time. When it is dark, Polly makes her mum come with her and stand outside with her torch in all weather. In winter it means putting hat coat scarves and gloves on to go to the toilet. The bathroom would come later. Polly, and everyone else, still bathe in a tin bath in front of the kitchen fire late at night.

Outside in the farmyard where once a large water cart stood in the centre for horses and cattle to drink from now is this mains water tank, and also one in the meadow by the gate where they all remember to take a drink when needed. These outside mains water drinking vessels would fill to the required level, adjusted with an automatic ball-cock like a toilet cistern.

Now with electricity installed also in farm buildings, everything is much easier to achieve, just reach for the switch each time when entering the building.

Father buys four Nissen huts from the MOD on an aerodrome nearby. There are aircraft bases all around the farm, both British and American. But after the war, all of this is coming to an end and not needed any more. Nissen huts have a rounded roof, and are a good size. On the farm, Father needs a large shed to accommodate the large implements that need to be kept in the dry, such as the seed drill. The intention is to store these, and more things that need to be kept dry.

While the building is in progress, lots of ladders, heavy pieces of wood, not to mention the curved galvanized sheets to complete the roofing; of course Polly is around, helping to do the jobs, handing the tools to whoever needs them, when suddenly a railway sleeper comes sliding towards her, hits her head, bounces off, and she is not feeling very happy about that. No broken bones or cuts or bruises, fortunately no bleeding, but still, we won't tell Mother. Surprisingly, it doesn't knock her down either. She is always told not to make noises, no crying, not in front of boys and men from the village. Yet another scrape with one of those lucky escapes.

Eventually when this large shed is finished, father has another idea, which is to put battery hens in to lay eggs, it is not a good idea, the poor hens don't get room to move staying in a small cage space, just enough to turn round when they lay the egg which rolls down in front of where their food and water is. They can always eat and drink, but without moving. The awful thing is, it is suggested to keep the lights on 24 hours, through the night, so the hen might possibly lay two or more eggs a day. It isn't kind to the hens, Polly's father is not happy with this, not good for the hens, and it is soon to be dispensed with. The chicks are soon back in open range in large pens, and roost at night in huts on perches, sitting and sleeping all in at nights, safely away from foxes, and in huge great pens, five or six thousand hens.

When her cousins come around on holiday, Polly is big enough to have a ride on the back of a motor bike if it's driven slowly. She is not too keen on it that much, it isn't something she wants to get used to.

This is the 1950s, when Polly is twelve, thirteen, fourteen, it isn't really known as the teens.

In these times, children, girls, of this age don't have special fashions in clothes, make up or lots of sensational times, children aren't catered for, or as in later years known as teenagers. Whether you are a girl or a boy, there are no special events or glamourous happenings for your age, it is just clothes, made in similar style to mother's and father's grown up clothes and shoes. There is nothing designed for young people in their teens, so Polly has to be content to be a young lady and the boys are young men. They have all to behave in a dignified way.

Young Lady Polly

Polly absolutely loves getting her riding habit and jodhpurs and hacking jacket, and setting off with father to the Michaelmas farm sales. This is from about October 10th after the harvest, all the corn is gathered in, then it is the time for exchanges of farm workers, farmers selling up all their machinery and animals. It is the time between autumn and winter, and many agricultural workers are moving to new farms to work and live. Most farms have tied cottages alongside the farm ready to accommodate their workers. It is wonderful to go along with father to meet all the other farmers at the sales and sometimes see the inside auctions.

It is really special for Polly, having a programme of all the items for sale and pricing them as they are sold! There is livestock, horses, cattle, bullocks and heifers, milking cows and baby calves. Also, earlier in the summer they go to the Royal Norfolk Agricultural Show. This is a really special event, definitely worth getting dressed up for.

Hundreds and hundreds of tents are set up by the marketing companies that sell animal food, all suppliers of machinery and everything that a farmer needs, there is a grand ring where all the exhibits come, special competitions for best classes of horses, cows, bulls, sheep, lambs, pigs and so on. Polly's parents have never missed a year as this happens annually. It's one of the biggest events where so many people came together.

Polly's uncle, her dad's brother, Uncle Dick, has, one particular year, been honoured to be commissioned to provide the flowers and bedding plants for the President's Tent, of which he is so very proud. He has grown special red salvias, and small bedding plants that adorn the royal boxes around the President's Tent. Polly, together with her parents, are guests in the President's Tent for a grand midday luncheon attended by HM QEII and Prince Phillip who are at the head table of course. To dine in the presence of the royal family is such an honour, and only the smartest clothes to be worn. There could be eighty or a hundred people attending that particular day, for a silver service luncheon. Polly feels very smart indeed in a floral cotton dress.

Of course, it is the very best food, prepared and cooked, fit for the queen and her guests. There are one or two speeches, but Polly isn't very interested. When the luncheon is over she attends the Grand Ring where there are displays of horsemanship, motor cycle displays, pony races, a gymkhana, a man diving into a tub of water with fire surrounding it, everything is so very exciting, and nobody wants to leave. The whole event is so very well managed. Hundreds of people have turned up to this occasion each and every year since 1847, it is a two-day event. Always the school children are there, and many stewards, that can be seen wearing bowler hats. Everyone is in there, from the lords and ladies right down to the ordinary farm worker, with his wife and children if he can afford. Where the tents are, there is often coffee, tea and a piece of cake for trade customers. There are also dogs and rabbits and other small animals shown at this event.

Hobnail boots

Another favourite thing of Polly's is to wear her hobnail boots. She is about fourteen or fifteen years of age, and has the urge to wear her boots like the boys. Really it is extra protection for her feet and ankles whilst on the farm, and also helpful when walking along the rough driveway and farmyard surface. They are also good for riding, but there are no nails in the soles of her boots.

She feels like a real farmer in those boots, going around the Michaelmas farm sales, and also on Fridays at the Corn Exchange where Polly tales a sample of the corn, wheat or barley that has been harvested this and every year. Off she goes to do the business for her father amongst all these men, farmers and corn merchants, three or four hundred of them. She's the only female, quite happy to do father's bidding, and she does feel special in her boots. She doesn't want to get them spoilt at any cost!

A Stack of Wheat

At fifteen, Polly is now attending all the functions and events with her parents, and doing more on the farm. Her father is particularly fond of a beautiful stack of hay that he and Polly had have built.

Her father is very anxious to get the thatch put on securely, so that the damp won't get in, it has been built with much precision by both father and daughter. Polly is about to have her first lesson in thatching when a representative from one of the animal feed companies arrives, and he happens to have a hobby of photography.

"Please allow me to photograph your daughter, at her first attempt at this new and extremely clever art of thatching."

He takes a picture, and off he goes, and the next month to everyone's amazement, the very photo appears on the front of the Farmer's Weekly magazine, proof of Polly's independence and lack of fear of heights – or anything else.

AFTER ONE LESSON

After her first lesson in thatching given by her father, 16-year-old Miss June Ford seems to be making a capable job of it. Miss Ford works for her father Mr. B. V. Ford, Bridge Green Farm, Burston, near Diss, Norfolk.

Bridge Green Farm Girl

About the Author

Caroline Simmons grew up on Bridge Green Farm at Burston near Diss. Her father, the son of a farmer, had been a pupil at the famous Burston Strike School. Both her grandmothers were suffragettes and she was encouraged to be independent and curious from an early age. Her adventures on the farm are only a small part of her story, and she is looking forward to sharing more.

14482226R00063

Printed in Poland
by Amazon Fulfillment
Poland Sp. z o.o., Wrocław